To Love and Be Loved

Secrets of Intimacy

Rev. John C. Tormey

Liguori Publications
One Liguori Drive
Liguori, Missouri 63057
(314) 464-2500

Imprimi Potest:
Edmund T. Langton, C.SS.R.
Provincial, St. Louis Province
Redemptorist Fathers

Imprimatur:
St. Louis, October 11, 1978
+ John N. Wurm, S.T.D., Ph.D.
Vicar General, Archdiocese of St. Louis

ISBN 0-89243-093-1

Grateful acknowledgment is extended for use of quotations
from the *Good News Bible* — New Testament: Copyright ©
American Bible Society 1966, 1971, 1976. Used by permission.

I am happy to dedicate
these reflections to
Katie, Sean, Shannon, and Jean
who inspire the sharing and caring
of true intimacy.

Table of Contents

Introduction

Intimacy is that wonderful feeling that comes from knowing that someone is Number One in your life, that someone is deeply concerned about what is happening to you, that someone appreciates what you enjoy and respects what you hold as very sacred.

Intimacy has so often been mistaken for sex that it is time to spell out its meaning more clearly. Actually, it is quite difficult to define. It is far easier to describe it by its qualities, for it happens only after two people have fulfilled many other needs. It takes a great deal of hard work and personal sacrifice.

What, then, are some of the characteristics of intimacy? Perhaps the following reflections will help you arrive at a comfortable definition, stir your imagination for more sensitive sharing, create some dreams that you never thought possible, guide your conscience in times of trouble, and help you keep some of those promises you always make.

To Love and Be Loved

Secrets of Intimacy

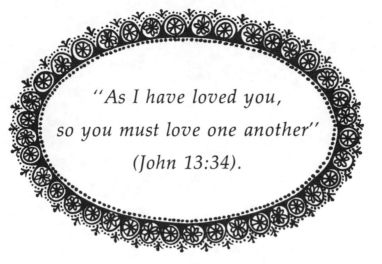

"As I have loved you,
so you must love one another"
(John 13:34).

Jesus gave his life for those he loved. Giving your life for the person you love will not call for the martyrdom of death but, rather, the margin of living you share with your loved one. Laying down your life means giving your time, your attention, and the fullness of your presence. It means not using words like "inconvenience" or "interruption" when the person you love needs you.

FULL

MOST VALUABLE & HARDEST ASSET TO GIVE

Caring

Intimacy is a caring experience. "Caring," rather than loving, seems to be a better word these days. "Love" has gone commercial with slogans such as "Cats love Cat Chow" and "Your hearty appetite will love our hamburger." Let the poets talk of love and entertainers sing of its glory; but if you wish to experience true intimacy, concentrate on the patience, prudence, and inconvenience of caring.

Essential to caring is the awesome experience of devotion. One of the finest compliments I have *100% commitment* heard about a relationship was the simple remark, "They are so devoted to each other." Devotion means putting a premium value on a person so that nothing or no one is ever more important.

The word devotion comes from the Latin *devotio,* which means "consecration." When you care for someone you consider that person sacred, and it becomes a sacrilege to desecrate that person with ridicule or rudeness.

Time Together

Intimacy offers many precious gifts, but perhaps the most important is the simple gift of time. Time means waiting, listening, being attentive and fully present to the other. One hour of quality time in undistracted conversation can be worth endless hours of watching television — when both persons are almost totally oblivious to each other.

Benjamin Franklin called time "the stuff of life." When two people in love pledge their lives to each other — even to the point of giving up their lives — their thoughts must turn to giving up their time for each other. Every day should have a scheduled block of time that is sacred for personal interaction. Perhaps the nice weather will suggest an after-dinner stroll or the simple enjoyment of listening attentively to each other.

Time also implies the proper distribution of energy. If you save the time but are always exhausted, you might be spending those minutes and hours getting on each other's nerves. Arrange your priorities and do not tire yourself out with activities that tend to separate you.

"Do Nothing" Days

Intimacy enjoys "do nothing" days, when you clear the calendar and refuse to let anything interfere with your mutual relaxation. Allow spontaneity to dictate your desires. Simply enjoy being together. You will be surprised how much tension you will relieve and how nice it is to daydream and do nothing.

Perhaps you can make it a seasonal experience: a long walk in a winter wonderland of snow; a spring curiosity trip to quaint shops; a summer day at a quiet beach or park where few people trespass; an autumn hike up a mountain, with a knapsack of wine and cheese. Whenever and wherever, be sure to schedule a date and have a special place that gives you serenity for a "do nothing" day.

"Being" and "knowing" are as important as "doing" and "having"; yet so many people in love feel uncomfortable or bored just being with one another and getting to know each other. They have to be *doing* something. But their very activity hinders them from attaining intimate knowledge of each other.

Enriching Experiences

Intimacy cannot survive a greedy attachment to money. The lover who is always putting a price tag on enriching experiences is a bore, especially when the money is only enhancing a savings account. Prudence and financial responsibility should guide your spending, but it is foolish to pass up a good time because of stinginess.

The secret of spending money is to enjoy the most from the least, so that you have some money left over for future enjoyment. Security is fine; but if it entombs you in boredom, take the risk and trade your money for creative leisure and vacation experiences. Fun times do wonders for intimacy.

Money is somewhat similar to fertilizer. If it stays in a pile its odor is unbearable. If it is spread around, it gives life, growth, and sustaining strength to the blossoming trees and flowers. Money can do the same for your relationship. It offers interesting and exciting experiences which help you to grow strong together.

Priorities

Intimacy finds and makes time for the beloved. When you truly love someone you say so; you don't just wait until all your work is done and you have nothing else to do.

Lovers take the time for a telephone call that simply says: "Honey, I'm thinking of you." They send a card or some flowers for no special reason except to say: "I miss you."

Intimacy is loyal to the principle of priority. There are many exciting experiences that could, and sometimes must, take a great deal of your time and attention. But if your beloved cannot share the joy, you should maintain a proper proportion which does not interfere with your love relationship.

Love Pilgrimage

Intimacy does not play the game of "hard to get" — expecting the beloved to pursue a wild and jealous chase through a maze of excuses and crazy experiences. Like most dangerous chases, two things can happen: either a person cracks up or simply halts the pursuit.

If you really care, stop your wild ego trip and let your lover come close. Save your energy by pooling your love; live this short life together. Chasing one another only makes you tired and tense.

The pilgrimage of love can be wonderful when both partners go hand in hand in the same direction and at an even tempo. Then life becomes a scenic route, where both can stop off to rest and simply enjoy the experience of being together.

Respect for Privacy

Intimacy respects privacy. Lovers need to retreat into their aloneness and experience feelings that they share with no one else. It is impossible — even for lovers — to share everything of themselves. There should be an area in all where no one trespasses and no explanations are necessary.

Aloneness is not an escape from your beloved; rather, it is a new venture into the depth of your relationship, which gives resonance to the experiences you share together. It seeks detachment for the purpose of self-discipline, so that you can give yourself totally in love.

Sharing intimacy and ideas with your spouse presumes that you are in touch with your own soul. That attention and appreciation come only when you are alone. Privacy gives you time to find the roots of your feelings; a person without roots can easily become superficial and ruthless.

Importance of Solitude

Intimacy knows that reaching out comes from being secure within. If inner alienation impedes your thinking and your feeling, the resulting confusion is sure to keep you hung up on yourself. The stronger your sense of identity, the deeper you will experience intimacy, because you will be reaching out instead of looking within.

"Getting it together" is the contemporary term for harmonizing your ideas and "gut" feelings. If your mind is a mess and your emotions are erratic, the problem is with you and not the relationship.

"Smooth runs the water where the brook is deep." Solitude is the opportunity to venture deeper into your soul and get everything together. It is that necessary time to stop and think, to organize and assimilate your life into one unified pattern. Only then are you a secure and serene person to love. Without solitude you risk the chance of always being confused.

Mind Enrichment

Intimacy recognizes that enriching your mind increases your value to your beloved. If you are rich with ideas and wealthy with wit and wisdom, your conversation will be stimulating and enjoyable. It is always nice to live, love, learn, and laugh with a person who is intelligent.

Invest in your mind by reading and devoting yourself to self-education. Motivate yourself with the honest axiom: "I know that I do not know." Do not pass up any opportunity to broaden your horizons or deepen your knowledge. You will free yourself from pettiness and escape the torturous boredom which stifles so many love relationships.

Exciting conversation starts in the mind. So, if you are dull and boring and cannot communicate with your beloved, work on the source of your problem — your mind. Knowledge not only makes you more exciting to be with but also sharpens your insight and perception, so that you have a greater capacity for understanding. Somewhat like a bank account, the more ideas you put into your mind, the greater the interest.

Anniversaries

Intimacy remembers anniversary times: birthdays, the day you met, the day you were married. They come up just when you seem to need them — to culminate your joy or to stifle your pride. They offer you sacred, sensitive times to forgive failures, forget hurt feelings, and to start fresh with new promises.

An anniversary day can be your inventory accounting day. Tally up your gifts. Count your blessings. Evaluate your experiences. Discard the products of your pride and selfishness which overload your love with too many impediments. Inventory time is your chance to simplify life and to restore order.

If there is one day you should save for dinner, dancing, and romance, let it be the anniversary day. You will look forward to it on each occasion and enjoy the promises you'll make for another happy time.

II

*"Love is patient
and kind"
(1 Corinthians 13:4).*

Intimacy transports the lover into the sacred zone of the beloved's soul. This is an area which is extremely vulnerable to sarcasm, ridicule, and any type of harshness. Kindness is the only virtue strong enough to protect you from the tensions, disappointments, and disagreements which may incline you to destroy what is sacred in your beloved.

Sensitive Listening

Intimacy is always cautious to exchange ideas and feelings with accuracy, so that both people have the same facts. Saying exactly what you mean and allowing time for understanding will insure that the message sent is the same message that is received.

Little techniques, like starting the conversation with the personal name, sitting down to talk and looking straight at each other, help to prevent deadly apathy. Too many important decisions are made on the run. Taunting remarks disrupt harmony and hinder understanding.

Intimacy patiently listens to the entire message and then looks at it in proper perspective. It does not hurry to comment and clarify. Where is the message coming from — is your beloved hurt, hung up, or helpless? Sensitivity always listens to the feelings behind the words.

Good Timing

Intimacy does not proceed with reckless disregard for timing by saying the wrong thing at the wrong time in the wrong place. Good timing is usually a matter of courteous consideration. Often lovers are offended not so much by what is said as by how it is said, when it is said, and where it is said.

There is a time to deliver your opinion, your constructive criticism, and even to show your anger; but a loving person seeks the best opportunity after sufficient preparation and the right choice of words to insure understanding. Of course, good timing never takes the risk of publicly ridiculing the beloved with needless outbursts of anger.

Good timing means that you don't create a problem just as you are going out to a party or an evening of entertainment. Good timing does not spoil a special day or further aggravate an already difficult day. There will be a time later on to give your opinion, and perhaps by that time the problem will have resolved itself or it simply will not be as important any more.

Problem Solving

Intimacy realizes that mustering mistakes from the past only hampers an amicable solution to the present problem. Reminding each other of humiliating, humorless incidents of the past only insures a greater surge of anger or deeper withdrawal. Remember, even a criminal cannot be tried for the same crime a second time.

Here are four ways to build up a better relationship: forgive, forget, start fresh, and move forward. If you have the capacity to forgive, time will help you forget. If you initiate a fresh new start, love will move you forward.

Make a pact with the person you love to leave disagreements buried in the past. Remember, the person who has to dig up the "dirt" of the past to bury a present disagreement is usually losing ground.

Crisis of Change

Intimacy softens the blow of necessary change. With courtesy and gradual compromise, it tempers the trauma of surprise coming from new choices made. All new plans require fresh promises and patient understanding.

Every uncharted course presents a different priority and affects the proportion of time and attention you give the person you love. If the balance of love is to remain stable, intimacy must dissolve the old and embrace the new. Too many irons in the same fire dissipate the warmth of love.

Before changing your mind, consider the consequences. If the choice is a new career which leaves your beloved alienated and alone, intimacy has been exposed to a poor choice. In that case, is change worth the inevitable crisis?

Gentle Silence

Intimacy realizes that a displeasure avoided brings as much happiness as a pleasure received. If, by diplomacy, you can defuse an explosive disagreement, you will prevent many an embarrassing "blow up."

When the situation does not call for a response, take a large gulp and swallow your pride. Allow your beloved the time and space to sound off. Often the echo chamber of your silence makes the one-sided argument sound quite foolish, and peace prevails because there is no opposition.

Whatever is temporal is tolerable. You can put up with a little heartache if you know that you are avoiding a violent disagreement and that soon peace will be restored. Ask yourself: "Is my disagreement or argument worth all the effort? Is the gain worth the pain?" Sometimes you should express your opinion and suffer the agony of conflict because the situation is serious and important. There are many other occasions, however, which dictate the courage of a listening and gentle silence.

Sense of Humor

Intimacy knows that even the most strategic plans and artistic dreams will occasionally meet disappointment and disillusionment. No one is to blame. That is just the way life unfolds. It is foolish to lash out against the person you love, blaming him or her for the setback. It is even worse to recede into a melancholy mood which is always a symptom of selfishness.

In such a situation, intimacy relies on a sense of humor which implies detachment from self-seeking and provides the ability to laugh at the incongruities of life. A sense of humor keeps the problem in perspective, the response always patient, the mind on the move for new arrangements, and the relationship still pleasant without unnecessary criticism.

Blaming each other only wastes precious time. Laughter and preparation for an alternative plan often bring two people even closer together. Lovers who can laugh at themselves have faith in themselves. They know that every problem has a solution and that a little laughter will often uncover the answer more quickly than criticism or self-pity.

III

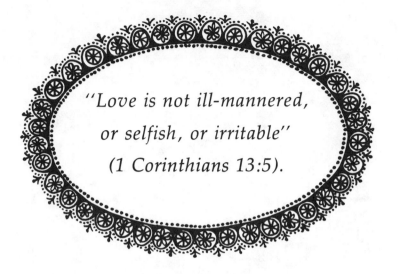

*"Love is not ill-mannered,
or selfish, or irritable"*
(1 Corinthians 13:5).

The operative word in intimacy is giving. Most problems occur when lovers want to get more than they wish to give. Rudeness, revenge, and ill-humor are all symptoms of selfishness. Lovers place into each other's hands the power to inflict pain. Even intimacy has its disagreements. Do you have the capacity to analyze and heal hurt feelings? This is the true test of intimacy — to begin again when it seems love has been lost.

Rudeness

Intimacy is not rude and selfish. It does not mumble monosyllables through a newspaper in response to a lover's exciting news or distressing heartaches.

Intimacy does not annihilate the other with devastating words. Nor does it ignore serious ideas with sarcastic laughter. Never does it resort to name-calling, even in private. And, of course, it never exposes the beloved to public ridicule.

The more closely personal you become with your loved one, the more generous you are with courtesy and kindness. A sensitive person is always quick to listen, even quicker to understand, and is quickest to relieve pain and heal hurt feelings.

Forgiveness

Intimacy implies the capacity to heed and heal hurt feelings. It allows no room for anger and anxiety to spoil a nice day. Peace does not happen by itself. Someone must desire it first and take the courageous step to make it happen. There are times when "love *is* having to say you are sorry." When two persons who really love each other have quarreled, both should be eager to make the first apology.

Life is so short and love is so fascinating. You should, then, spend your time in sharing your mutual joys and in giving your total love to the person who is most important to you. Quarrels only waste your limited supply of time and healthy life.

Intimacy is always ready to forgive, forget, and start anew. With the wisdom of St. Paul it looks to the future: "The one thing I do . . . is to forget what is behind me and do my best to reach what is ahead" (Philippians 3:13).

Silent Treatment

Intimacy does not punish others with deliberate isolation — either by total disregard or by cold monosyllabic responses. Nothing frustrates a person more than to be considered a "nothing."

The musical refrain "Silence like a cancer grows" offers the best description of this type of behavior. The silent treatment strikes at the life line of love. It eats away at the dignity of love.

Time is so valuable, life is so short, and love is so admirable that the silent treatment should never be adopted by those who say they still care.

Constructive Criticism

Intimacy does not protract constructive criticism with long and boring analysis. It does not overkill with continuous repetition of harmful, consequences. Constant audio replay of another's mistake will only insure anger and assure aggravation.

Allow the mistake to mellow, and work out the analysis quietly in your mind before rendering any qualitative judgment. Select your words prudently, deliver them patiently, and listen attentively. Whatever you have to say, say it calmly, say it firmly, but say it only once.

Then let your body language continue the conversation — with a smile and perhaps a huge hug. Endearment and affection do wonders for constructive criticism. Finally, trust your beloved, and allow the wisdom of your advice to gently percolate without nagging for instant results.

Game Playing

Intimacy does not feign headaches, pretend fainting spells, or simulate nervous breakdowns — all to frighten the beloved with guilt feelings. A threat of suicide, of course, is the worst power play of all: "Meet my demands or else you will have to live with the guilt of my death for your life."

Gentle persuasion and sound reason are still the best vehicles of communication for two people who truly wish to understand each other and be free from the agony of resentment. Games and dramatic performances are deceitful because they undermine trust and respect.

Agree to disagree, but avoid being disagreeable. Allow your beloved to be different. The pressure of "tricks or treats" often culminates in "Halloween horrors."

Soft Answer

Intimacy understands that a person often strikes out in anger to relieve the pain and irritation of frustration. Instead of concentrating on the angry words, lovers should focus their attention on finding the cause of the problem.

Evaluating rather than judging behavior can offer better alternatives for the future. Ask yourself some questions: "What is making my beloved so frustrated? Is it something I do? Are gentle words not forthcoming because I do not listen? Am I taking the time to understand the feelings involved? Do I show by my attitude that I consider my beloved unimportant?"

Anger is a symptom of something boiling and steaming in the depth of the soul. Intimacy reaches into a person's frustration and releases the pressure that is causing the anger. Once the pressure is shut off, the steam dissipates and the soul enjoys the serenity which brings a smile of relief and overtures of reconciliation.

Unfunny Humor

Intimacy does not aggravate a person with practical jokes which exhibit a touch of the sadistic. Most often, the laughter is cruel and the rhetorical question "Can't you take a joke?" does not deserve an answer.

An anonymous wise person once wrote: "When everyone cannot join in the laughter, when someone sacred is made to appear comical, and when some heart carries away an ache, then it is a poor joke." When you love someone, reverence is more important than laughter.

When your sense of humor lacks finesse and fairness, you may have humor but you have no sense. The person with a genuine sense of humor is always uplifting, and makes serious people aware and appreciative of the light side of life.

Frustration

Intimacy never pushes others so far that they have nothing to lose by leaving. There is a limit to the amount of frustration and pain that can be endured. Once that limit is reached, even ardent lovers will seek other less frustrating and more enjoyable ways of satisfying their needs.

People who play Russian roulette with the emotions of others eventually lose. Your partner will ordinarily recover from the emotional injury you have inflicted. But there will come a time when your continuing foolishness will "blow" your lover's mind, and love will not respond to the resuscitation of hugs and kisses.

Love is such a precious and delicate gift that it is foolhardy to continue giving it to a person who does not seem to care. Love is never lost suddenly and without warning. It usually dies from abuse. The heart simply has nothing left to restore itself. And, in most cases, it finds someone else to love.

Ridicule

Intimacy avoids being the cause of emotional pain. How can anyone, out of spite, cause a loved one to worry and weep?

Knowledge is power. When lovers reveal their weaknesses to each other, they surrender potentially destructive powers. Intimacy does not abuse these revelations by resorting to sly ridicule or crushing criticism.

Intimacy lives by the golden rule: "Do unto others what you wish them to do unto you." Any reasonable person certainly can understand that rendering pain only adds fuel to the fire of disagreement. Intimacy asks the rhetorical question: "Would I be hurt if my beloved did this to me?"

Penny-pinching

Intimacy realizes that the best feelings arise when lovers do enjoyable things together. They share their wealth in order to share special days with each other.

If you do not make plans and promises, time has a way of passing you by with some of life's greatest experiences. There are no excuses. You always have time for what you think is important. Enjoying fun-filled days are far more important than getting things done that keep you apart.

The money sits in the bank and you sit at home. Only the money gains interest; you get bored. Invest in vacations and exciting experiences that enrich your love. Intimacy is invaluable, so do not be afraid of the price tag. It will be your most precious possession when you review your life on your deathbed.

IV

"Love is not happy with evil,
but is happy with the truth"
(1 Corinthians 13:6).

Truth is the backbone of trust. When the backbone is diseased with deceit, love goes limp in pain and soon wastes away. Lying cripples freedom; there is always worry about the cover-up and eventual discovery. Listen to the wisdom of Jesus: ". . . the truth will make you free" (John 8:32).

Truthfulness

Intimacy knows that one lie leads to another, and there is always the possibility of eventually being caught. Lying severs the artery of love, which is trust. When two people cannot trust each other, they lose mutual respect. And with this loss, love diminishes and finally disappears.

Evils that occur in a love relationship — infidelity, excessive drinking and gambling, careless use of money, and other failings — breed on lies. But perhaps the most devastating lie is the one that plays games with semantics to protect pride and power. It is so very hard to be concerned about and sensitive to a person who is always "bending the truth" to defend the indefensible. The lover who plays these games with words makes the beloved look like a fool. And this, of course, only causes frustration and resentment.

A lie brought the first couple, Adam and Eve, their extreme unhappiness. And today, lies constantly cause a crisis in the trust bond of any relationship. The pain which comes from the truth can be healed and time will forget it; but a lie will never heal and time will not accept it.

Keeping Promises

Intimacy does not make a promise that it has no intention of keeping. "You are as good as your word" and "Your word is your trust" are two axioms that can remind you of the importance of consistency, consideration, and confidence. Promises are the common denominators of trust. Be true to your word, even if it requires great personal sacrifice.

The lover who is always dipping deep into the grab bag of excuses and singing the refrain, "That is not what I said. I said: maybe, perhaps, possibly . . .," frustrates and angers the beloved. Breaking promises is the surest way to break another's spirit.

Place your promises on a priority list by keeping a calendar of your plans. Good intentions with no follow-through can become quite disgusting. If you cannot keep a promise, either because of your own limitations or emergency circumstances, be honest and straightforward with your explanation and work out a mutually agreeable and alternative arrangement.

Sharing Ideas

Intimacy seeks to share great ideas and introduce new experiences to the person who is loved. Love implies a mutual teaching and learning exchange. Two people in love need each other to broaden visions and reach horizons.

Sharing ideas, however, implies that there is no absolute pressure for acceptance and perfect conformity. Each should be allowed to take the best and leave the rest. Sharing seeks improvement, but only with the other's approval.

Intimacy certainly does not mean that your beloved must accept your philosophy of life or attend always to your opinions. If you expect to inspire and uplift your loved one, allow your sincerity to gain respect; and time will achieve your dream. Share your opinions with the awesome wish of Teilhard de Chardin: "May you find the path which will lead you to the highest and truest of yourself!"

Showing Reverence

Intimacy shuns vulgarity and sarcasm. It treats the loved one with dignity and respect, ever careful to avoid causing embarrassment.

The more intimate your love, the greater the need for courtesy and sensitivity. Because your beloved is sacred, reverence is due.

You love the divine light within your beloved. That light will continue to shine throughout life, and even after death. If you are inclined to whisper in admiration: "She's divine," "He's out of this world," then you are right. The spirit of each of you is a spark of divinity, and sarcasm is a sacrilege disgracing the holiness that abides within.

V

"Love never gives up:
its faith, hope, and patience
never fail"
(1 Corinthians 13:7).

Intimacy is an uplifting experience. When singers praise love as lifting them higher, they capture the soaring feeling of reaching to the height and length and breadth that love can bring. And the helium that lifts them up is trust and hope in the worth of the person loved.

Mutual Trust

Intimacy is a trust trip into the unknown; because it means surrendering heart and hand to another, while not really knowing how the trip will end. Will the journey lead to enchantment or disenchantment?

Lovers who give themselves to each other in a spirit of trust cannot predict the future their promises will bring. But when they respect the power and sacredness of their promises without fear of consequences, they assure their future because they are riding "the trust train" which travels in the right direction.

The trust trip brings you through tunnels of darkness guided by the honest enlightenment of your loyalty. It can be the thrill ride of your life if you both keep your eyes open to avoid the pitfalls that derail promises and demolish trust.

Peaceful Living

Intimacy disdains a spirit of rivalry. It realizes that developing personal potential does not revolve around senseless competition. Achieving a goal is worthless if it destroys the self-esteem of the beloved.

Lovers do not worry about winners and losers. Their concern is mutual enjoyment. "Whatever you can do, I can do better" is never in their hearts or on their lips.

Intimacy is neither combat nor competition. It is compromise and cooperation, with heavy doses of tender loving care. The V sign should stand for peace not victory. The tension resulting from trying to outdo your beloved will only destroy the trust that sustains intimacy.

Sound Sentiment

Intimacy does not think that sentiment is silly. Poetic refrains and pleasant reflections should be bolstered with emotional words: "I love you, I need you, I miss you."

Sentiment keeps a relationship sacred. Anniversaries become holy days, romantic memories temper insane arguments with a recall to sanity, and "sweet nothings" awaken a new promise of attention and affection.

When lovers lose sentiment, they can easily become cold, cautious, and eventually care-less. Sentiment keeps you appreciative; it enhances the desire to enjoy the scents, sounds, and softness that keep you thrilled with each other.

Living the Present

Intimacy does not make constant comparisons. There are enough differences in people to assure disillusionment in this way. Better to simply appreciate the best qualities of the other person, and leave the rest to oblivion.

Set yourself free from this futile frustration by forgetting how others made you happy, and direct your attention only on your beloved. Let go of the memories with others, and make new memories with the person who is making you happy now.

Lovers live intensely for today and absorb the beauty of each other. So let go of your past, enjoy the present, and anticipate the future.

VI

"Love one another warmly . . . be eager to show respect for one another" (Romans 12:10).

Intimacy is basically a spiritual experience. If two minds do not touch affectionately, two bodies will eventually suffer frigidity and frustration. Often when two lovers find it difficult to communicate their thoughts they have problems with sexual compatibility. Making love should be a warm expression of patience, tenderness, imagination, and appreciation. It should create and culminate in sexual happiness which reflects the awesome spiritual feeling of caring.

Warmth

Intimacy knows that the best thaw to a freeze is warmth. If your beloved is giving you the cool treatment, turn on the warmth of your endearment and affection. Ordinarily, lovers cannot resist the thaw and will seek reconciliation.

What does the cool treatment gain for you? Only "wasted days and wasted nights," which make you feel like a fool when you finally realize what you have done to each other. In most cases, you have spoiled some special moments of sharing and lost some ecstatic memories.

Intimacy respects the ancient proverb: "If you know what hurts you, then you know what hurts others." If you have ever felt the pain of the cool treatment, how could you ever treat with disdain the one you love?

Affection

Intimacy stays "in touch." The tender touch of affection is an unmistakable sign of belonging. It makes a person feel worthwhile and accepted. Of course, it does wonders for communication; its vibrations spell out what words cannot adequately express.

Affection also initiates the beautiful language leading to forgiveness and reconciliation. Wordlessly, it heals hurt feelings and turns back anger.

Affection's warmth and sensitivity are precious gifts for any lover's personality. It is so very difficult to be cold, cunning, and calculating when you are inclined to embrace with a hug and kiss.

Carefree Time

Intimacy is spontaneous and impulsive. It plans outings on the spur of the moment. Natural appreciation for beauty and the excitement of sharing keep preparations to an absolute minimum. Boredom does not have a chance when two people simply enjoy being together.

The place can be anywhere — a beach, a mountain, a bicycle path. The important ingredient of intimacy is time. It actually stares out of the word: in-*tim*-acy.

When two people commit their lives to each other they also commit their time. They can run short of giving time to clients, clubs, and crusades but never to each other. They work together to get time together.

Fond Glances

Intimacy is captured by the German idiom: *"Ich seh dich gern,"* which means "I see you fondly." The eyes are the windows of the soul, and when love is warm and glowing they sparkle with delight.

Eyes invite intimacy with a warm glance, a hidden wink — evidences of tender compassion. What the lips fail to express, the eyes cannot hide. Eyes also save lovers from angry statements — with love "vibes" rather than vile words.

When you "see each other fondly," the sweet scent of love is intensified, and your relationship is saved from mediocrity. Remember, "Out of sight" can mean "out of mind," which may lead to "out of love."

Special Memories

Intimacy appreciates the fact that experiences are passing but memories are forever. That is why it keeps a journal of love experiences and never apologizes for being sensitive and sentimental. Whether in a diary, a scrapbook, or a photo album, lovers store up special memories for future reference.

Intimacy evokes two premium words: special and sacred. Lovers have a special song, a favorite flower, a pleasant place to excite old memories. Every day is somehow special for lovers. Both the sunrise and sunset arouse special thoughts about the person loved.

When you respect each other as persons very sacred, it is easy to understand how everything can be considered "special." If you think that is romantic nonsense, get ready for boredom, and expect the anguish of living a very "unspecial" life.

Becoming Yourselves

Intimacy loves not only the "now" person but also the person "to be." Every person is in the transitional state of becoming. If lovers experience some present disappointment with each other, they must continue to affirm positive self-concepts. Then their dreams of the future will come true.

Intimacy never allows lovers to make snap judgments. It leaves room for both to develop their truest and best selves. Inconsiderate criticism, thoughtless ridicule, and petty put-downs stifle the becoming process.

Lovers recognize in each other a good and genuine person who is capable of becoming ever more loving. Today's loving attention and gentle persuasion augur well for tomorrow. Patience now will bring a glowing future. "The best is yet to come" for lovers who allow each other to become themselves.

The Secret of Being Loved
by Earnest Larsen

Alienated, afraid to love and be loved, too insecure to let others into their walled-in hearts: that is the way many people face each day. Larsen sensitively tells of real people who had been afraid, but boldly overcame their fears to find the beauty of human caring. Written for those who will risk their innermost security to find the secret of loving and being loved. Formerly a soft-cover picture book, *Hey! I Love You. Is That Okay? 64 page booklet,* $1.00.

Six Levels of a Happy Marriage
by Rev. Medard Laz

Can a troubled marriage be saved? Can a happy marriage become closer? The author, who has worked with hundreds of couples seeking deeper marriages, answers YES. He compares marriage to the tree of life in the Garden of Eden. Like Adam and Eve, we sometimes look for the fruit of the tree — the surface pleasures. Yet it is the *trunk of the marriage tree* that feeds the leaves and fruit — the trunk with its rings of friendship, sharing, and trusting. The author challenges couples to explore SIX levels of marriage — surface, physical, friendship, sharing, trusting, and nonverbal. A book for anyone who is married — or ever plans to be married. An excellent gift for newlyweds or engaged couples. *64 pages, soft cover,* only $1.00.